THE SECRET ADVANTAGE

SOUND WISDOM BOOKS BY EARL NIGHTINGALE

Lead the Field

The Direct Line

The Strangest Secret

Successful Living in a Changing World

Your Success Starts Here: Purpose and Personal Initiative

Transformational Living: Positivity, Mindset, and Persistence

Your Greatest Asset: Creative Vision and Empowered Communication

Master Your Inner World: Overcome Negative Emotions, Embrace Happiness, and Maximize Your Potential

THE STRANGEST SECRET SERIES

30 Days to Self-Confidence: A Guide to Stop Doubting Yourself and Start Succeeding

The Power of Goals: Timeless Lessons on Finding Purpose, Overcoming Doubt, and Taking Action

Habits for Success: The Pathway to Self-Mastery and Freedom

The Secret Advantage: Proven Principles for Financial Success

Succeeding in your finances, or in any other area of your life, is a matter of making a series of good decisions.

—JIM STOVALL,
Millionaire Answers

EARL NIGHTINGALE

THE SECRET ADVANTAGE

Proven Principles for Financial Success

THE STRANGEST SECRET SERIES

© Copyright 2025– Nightingale-Conant Corporation

All rights reserved. This book is protected by the copyright laws of the United States of America. No part of this publication may be reproduced, stored in or introduced into a retrieval system, or transmitted, in any form or by any means (electronic, mechanical, photocopying, recording or otherwise), without the prior written permission of the publisher. For permissions requests, contact the publisher, addressed "Attention: Permissions Coordinator," at the address below.

Published and distributed by:
SOUND WISDOM
P.O. Box 310
Shippensburg, PA 17257-0310
717-530-2122

info@soundwisdom.com

www.soundwisdom.com

While efforts have been made to verify information contained in this publication, neither the author nor the publisher assumes any responsibility for errors, inaccuracies, or omissions. While this publication is chock-full of useful, practical information; it is not intended to be legal or accounting advice. All readers are advised to seek competent lawyers and accountants to follow laws and regulations that may apply to specific situations. The reader of this publication assumes responsibility for the use of the information. The author and publisher assume no responsibility or liability whatsoever on the behalf of the reader of this publication.

The scanning, uploading and distribution of this publication via the Internet or via any other means without the permission of the publisher is illegal and punishable by law. Please purchase only authorized editions and do not participate in or encourage piracy of copyrightable materials.

ISBN 13 TP: 978-1-64095-503-5

ISBN 13 eBook: 978-1-64095-504-2

For Worldwide Distribution, Printed in the U.S.A.

1 2025

The only limits to your accomplishments in life are self-imposed.

—**DENIS WAITLEY**,
THE PSYCHOLOGY OF WINNING

CONTENTS

Introduction 11

1   Big Money 13

2   Big Plans 29

3   You Too? 43

4   95 to 5 Odds. 57

5   The Formula 73

6   Workable Formula Rules. 85

7   From Beginning-to-End Perspective 97

8   Establishing the Destination 113

About Earl Nightingale. 123

INTRODUCTION

by Vic Conant

My dad, Lloyd Conant, met Earl Nightingale in 1956 when Earl was a popular radio commentator on WGN in Chicago. At the time, Dad was a successful businessman, he owned his own direct marketing and printing company. Earl had just produced a recording titled *The Strangest Secret* and was looking for someone to market that product. The two of them met and Dad ended up selling a million of that recording over the years. These two men were a match made in Heaven. My dad the marketer and Earl the talent.

Earl, like Lloyd, was a "Great Depression" era child and grew up poor in California. Earl educated himself; he was an avid reader and a brilliant guy. Both had only a high school education. Earl was a totally self-made man as was my dad, so the two of them hit it off and eventually created Nightingale-Conant when I was about 14.

Every individual who has discovered what Earl Nightingale calls *The Strangest Secret* throughout the ages has found it to be a profoundly life-changing discovery. That secret? *You become what you think about*—and the fact that our thoughts *control* and many believe *create* our reality. Consequently, there is great responsibility placed on our thinking, making us responsible for our own future.

Vic Conant
Chairman of the Board
Nightingale-Conant Corporation

Note: *As Earl's wisdom was shared with audiences worldwide in the 1950s and 1960s, some statistics and other pertinent information have been updated as footnotes revealing the gravity of his teachings then—and how impactful and relevant they still are today.*

1

BIG MONEY

How would you like to make a million dollars? What do you want more than anything else in the world? How many times has some little voice within you told you to do or say something but you didn't do it or say it because you weren't sure you could believe in yourself?

If someone asked you to define the word *success*, how would you go about it? It's a fact that most people wouldn't know success if it kicked them right in the seat of the pants. I think it's best to stand at the starting line with nothing more than youth, strength, ambition, and determination. And then the game begins.

The 1950s were an excitingly phenomenal era called the Golden Age of American Capitalism, which is an apt description. During that time, more changes occurred, more progress was made than during any previous millennium in the development of humankind. It would be almost impossible to select the most important discovery in those recent years.

Just thinking is only daydreaming— the real challenge is learning how to think.

What would you choose? The jet engine, atomic energy, the new metal, synthetic fibers, rocket satellites, transistors, the laser, television, plastics, antibiotics, computers, men on the moon, self-image, psychology, mass communications? Well, the list goes on and on endlessly.

And if reflection on the recent past is amazing, what about the near future? No one can say for sure what changes will come during the next five or 10 years, but they will come—and they'll be amazing, even fantastic. The two most important areas of development in the future will be the collection of data for business and marketing and the study of the motivation of people. And that's what this book is all about.

The Secret Advantage focuses on success in the 21st century. Our changing world has never changed so rapidly as it's going to in the next few decades. During decades past and future I strongly submit to you that success of any kind boils down to just six words: *We become what we think about.* Just six words.

Those six words have been around for thousands of years in some form and spoken in every language known. We all know that just thinking is only daydreaming and the real challenge is to learn how to think. *The Secret Advantage* is based on core fundamentals to capitalize on your thoughts.

One problem business people have is that after developing and profiting from a good idea, they tend to stay with it in unchanging form too long. For some ventures that works, but for most, it won't. Plans and projects need updating on a regular annual basis. We need to ask ourselves at regular intervals a number of times each year, "How can we make it better, more efficient? How can we bring it up to the best of present, even future standards? And when we're creating or building something, are we anticipating the future?"

Technological revolution and globalization offer new ever-increasing challenges, so personal development skills are critical in any age. Competition today requires new types of leaders who understand the changing economic, cultural, and even social landscapes. But without the core competency to get the job in the first place and then to be able to rise to the top requires desire and tenacity.

For this reason, *The Secret Advantage* presents the information in four concise modules based on the word CORE. Used as an acronym for **C**ompetency, **O**pportunity, **R**esults, and **E**ffectiveness. Developing these dynamic core fundamentals begins with becoming competent in our career choices, industry, and specific field of expertise. Next, recognizing opportunities will get you to the top. And then anticipating successful results. The core skills and tactics are extremely effective in your unique qualifications.

The following information provides organized, life-changing principles for financial success, guaranteed. Let's start with focus.

16 The Secret Advantage

Focus

I'm sure you would agree that what you focus or concentrate on is what you bring into your life. I read something to the effect that many people fail to concentrate successfully because they think that concentration means willpower. They suppose that the harder they press, the faster they get through, but that's quite wrong.

Think of the photographic process. The secret of a clear picture lies in focus. You focus your camera lens steadily for the necessary length of time. Suppose I want to make a time exposure of a vase of flowers. I place them in front of the camera and keep them there. But suppose that after a few moments, I snatch away the vase and hold a book in front of the camera, and then snatch that away and hold up a chair and then put the flowers back for a few minutes. You know what will happen to the picture? It'll be a crazy blur.

That's what people do to their minds when they can't focus or keep their thoughts concentrated for any length of time. They think good thoughts for a few minutes, then they think sickness or fear. They think prosperity, and then they think depression. They think success and then failure. Is it any wonder that we are so apt to demonstrate a marred image of life?

It's always good to make a practical experiment to prove a point. So, I advise you to take one problem in your life and change your mind concerning it. Think about it

Big Money **17**

differently, see it in a different perspective. Keep focusing on that new way of thinking for a month, and you'll be astonished at the results. If you really do keep your thoughts on the new way of thinking, you won't have to wait a month for results. You will see how quickly that right thinking brings the right results.

But getting back to that excellent camera analogy. What you concentrate upon you bring into your life. So, what's important to you? What do you want more than anything else? Focus your mental lens on it and hold it until enough time has elapsed for it to be realized. Don't blur the picture with other nonessential wants or needs. Take one issue in your life, focus on it, and you'll be astonished at the results.

How much time and effort are you willing to give for what you think you want? And do you understand the truth that you get out of life just exactly what you put into it? Not a nickel more nor a nickel less.

Opportunity

The competitive landscape of our changing world creates unlimited opportunities. Some of the largest retailers today don't even own stores. Nightingale-Conant was the world's first and largest personal development publishing company. Lloyd Conant knew that if he had a product that can be mailed, it was a business. To date,

Nightingale-Conant has changed more lives and made more millionaires than all personal development authors and experts combined. The genesis of the company began with the audio program, *The Strangest Secret*, which was created to solve a problem.

In March 1956, an amazing thing happened. I was retiring from a very busy schedule and had decided to take it easy for a while in Arizona. Since I'd be away, the manager of one of my businesses asked me if I would record on tape a message he could play at the next sales meeting.

This made sense to me, so I decided to put a 30-minute talk in capsule form the important things I'd learned during the more than 20 years of research on why men and women succeeded or failed in life. I spent quite a bit of time putting it together, and then I recorded the message and called it *The Strangest Secret*. It wasn't long before people started asking for copies of the tape. Eventually we had it pressed into a record.

At first, hoping that I might get back the cost of producing it—the masters, pressings, the record jacket, the artwork, the plates, and all that—I just arbitrarily set a price of $15 on the record. I figured that helping people would be worth $15. And if it didn't help, they could certainly get their money back by returning it.

Well, to my amazement, *The Strangest Secret* started selling faster than ever. I soon had back my original investment, and immediately dropped the price on the record from $15 to $4.95. Then things really began to happen. My office had trouble keeping an adequate inventory. The record began to sell in the tens of thousands, and in a couple of years we'd sold more than a hundred thousand copies to companies and individuals and countries all worldwide.

I don't know whether you've ever had a bestseller on your hands or not, but I want to tell you it's just about the most interesting and exciting experience that can happen to a person. What pleased me most, of course, were the letters telling me that what I shared on the record was helpful in some way.

I had spent so many years wallowing in confusion that I knew how thrilling it was to get my life straightened out and on the right track for the first time. So I was happy to help others find that thrill as well. It's interesting about this business of living successfully—once you know how, it's a whole lot easier than living unsuccessfully. All the confusion, the running around in circles, the doubt and frustration disappear, and you can chart yourself a clear, straight course to what you want in life and achieve them with amazing regularity one after another.

I know one thing for sure, 95 percent of the people who feel they're hemmed in and held down by circumstances can achieve their goals one after another, right on schedule and get what they want out of life if they learn the secret advantage. And anyone can learn it, any child can learn it. It has been said that people don't need education as much as they need reminding. I think most people really know what they should do to achieve the things they want, but it's easy to forget what's important and to keep priorities in proper order.

It's Up to You

Living successfully and communicating more effectively with others are worthy goals. A company can back up employees with the finest product, the best reputation, outstanding advertising, and lots of support. But all that is behind you when you set about doing your job, your own work. At this point, it's up to you. You're as alone as a driver on the track at the Indianapolis 500. When you are performing your special skill, you are on your own when time to produce, to deliver the goods. And that's why we need to learn new ideas and be constantly reminded of old ones if we're going to compete successfully with those who do.

Why must we be reminded or find a way to remind ourselves of great ideas and new ways? Because our memories are short. In one respect, this is good in that we quickly forget our past mistakes, failures, and embarrassments. But it's bad in that we also tend to forget what we need to remember daily to achieve the results we want.

Living successfully is a whole lot easier than living unsuccessfully.

Return to the wisdom in this book again and again. Just a few minutes and you're back on the track again with a wealth of helpful ideas you can put into action immediately. No one can force an individual to improve, to become bigger and more effective. The person who moves forward has to do it through individual effort, and this is as it should be. Because in the last analysis, every person is working for themselves.

We are building our own lives regardless of where we happen to find our rewards. And the ideas and principles in this book provide you with an opportunity to grow, to live, and work closer to your potential as a human being.

What action you as an individual take is your own affair. And I believe that there isn't a human being on earth who's interested in growth and personal success who doesn't have these four vital needs:

1. Information

2. A plan of action to put that information to work

3. Constant reminding of priorities

4. Inspiration—the motivation to grow and build a better life! hope this book helps you move by leaps and bounds toward the goals you want to achieve.

Focus Points for Wealth & Wisdom

1. What do you focus on the most? What do you want more than anything else? What do you think about most often? Is the answer to all three questions the same? If not, why not?

Big Money **25**

2. *Are you getting out of life what you are putting into it?* What does that question mean to you? Does what you are putting into your life make it better or worse? Give an example of both. When I put _____ into my life, it makes it better because

_____

_____

_____

_____

_____

_____

_____

When I put _____ into my life, it makes it worse because

_____

_____

_____

_____

_____

_____

_____

3. How can you best put into practice CORE (Competency, Opportunity, Results, and Effectiveness) in your life, home, career?

_____

_____

_____

_____

_____

_____

_____

_____

_____

_____

_____

_____

_____

_____

_____

_____

_____

_____

_____

2

BIG PLANS

Do you have big plans to get rich? How big are your plans?

I urge you not to make little plans. There's nothing in little plans to stir your blood. But once a big idea is recorded, it never dies. If your daily life has become something of a bore, rather humdrum, or uninteresting, it could be because your plans are too small. More people would make bigger plans if they knew they could be accomplished. It takes courage to make big plans. True competency is built on habitual courage.

The people who stand out in history are those who had big plans that caught the fancy and imagination of others. A family with a big plan toward which they're working is a happy, busy, and interesting family. They suffer much less boredom and have no time for bickering or looking for convenient means of escape.

You might, just for fun, stop a minute and reevaluate your plans. What are they? What are you working toward? Is it big enough for you? Does it fill you with excitement

Big Plans **29**

when you think about it, and does it fill your days with energy and accomplishment? If not, maybe your plans are too small. Maybe you're trying to play it safe with your one chance at life here on earth.

All too often there's a wide gap between what a person started out to accomplish and what is actually accomplished. Usually, there are very good reasons for wanting to accomplish a particular goal. And it's usually your particular talents and abilities trying to get you on the right course. You are unlike any person who ever appeared on earth—but are you acting unique, or do you tend to act like other people? Do you go along to get along? There's no good reason for it.

What do you want or have more than anything else? If you can answer that question, you can discover the direction you should very probably take.

People accomplish what they set out to accomplish, but they often don't realize the extent of their own greatness and settle for less. They make their plans according to a misconception, taking their cues from those around them, assuming that what others do is right for them as well. Maybe it is, but maybe it isn't. Of one thing you can be sure—if your plan doesn't keep you interested and fill you with excitement at the prospect of its accomplishment, your plan is probably too small.

What is it that you really want to do? Why don't you do it? If it's good and hurts no one, go after it. You might be amazed at what you can do. You will discover the goals that come naturally to you do so for very good reasons—no one has a great big desire for something that is beyond your accomplishment.

Big Plans for Big Rewards

Owning a business or earning money from a job are both avenues to help you achieve wealth. There is a basic fundamental required in business for both employee and employer—*all the money you will ever make in the future is at this moment in the hands of someone else.* That's a law of nature like the law of gravity. If you are on top of a building and jump off, you will always go down. You will never go up. It's the same with all the laws of nature.

All the money you will ever make is at this moment in the hands of someone else. The challenge is to find a way to separate them from their money. Sure you could steal it, cheat them out of it, or maybe even inherit your fortune. However, there's only one way for the real winners in life to earn what you want as a competent and qualified professional. That is to *serve the customer.* Give extremely good service, and all the money you'll ever want to earn will come your way.

How much?

How would you like to earn a million dollars a year? Well, I can tell you how to do it, so get out your paper and pencil. All you have to do is figure out a way to earn

$2,739.75 a day, 365 days a year. Or if you don't like the idea of working on weekends, figure out a way to earn $19,230.76 a week. There's no allowance made for vacations or holidays, but maybe earning more than $19,000 a week would make you forget about vacations and holidays?

So how do you acquire a million dollars a year? Your answer—make $20,000 a week, and you can have a two-week vacation. Think of that.

Now, how do you go about earning $20,000 a week? Because earning a million dollars a year would make you rich, you should remember that there are really only four main ways of getting wealthy:

- One, have money working for you.
- Two, have people working for you.
- Three, have ideas working for you.
- Four, work for yourself.

Any one of these basic four reasons will produce results, or any combination.

Now let's get back to the $20,000 a week.

If you produced a product that could earn a $10 profit, and if you had dealers for this product in 200 cities, and if each dealer could sell two of these products a day, you would make a million dollars of profit. You see how it works?

32   The Secret Advantage

Or if you produced a product that could earn $1 of profit, you'd have to sell 20,000 of them a week. Right offhand, that might sound unreasonable, but it really isn't. It isn't easy, but it isn't impossible either. All you need is 20,000 regular customers subscribing to a good product or service for which you could earn $1 per week profit per customer. Of course, if you're not greedy and would be content to earn a half a million a year, you can cut those figures in half.

So don't say you don't know how to make a million dollars a year because I went to quite a bit of trouble to figure the whole thing out and pass it along to you. While certainly not all the money in the world, $20,000 a week is a tidy income, and with a little care and good judgment could easily take care of most ordinary expenses. As an exercise in creative thinking, why not spend time thinking of ways you could honestly earn a million dollars a year. If you only earned half that, it would be worthwhile.

In Business for Ourselves

Most people think the only way to become a multimillionaire is to own a business. Ownership does not guarantee success. There are many ways to become rich without owning a business. The truth is we are all in business for ourselves. If we work for a company, the products or services we are trusted to create are our products. The management, accountants, lawyers, coworkers, and most important, the customers are all tools of our trade, our business. They must be maintained and taken care of with competency. All jobs are important—there is no such thing as an unimportant job.

Every job in the world is important, if you think it's important and treat it as though it were important. There must be more than 10,000 different jobs, maybe a lot more, but each one can be very important if the person doing it treats it the right way.

We all know people who treat their work in an unimportant manner, who do just enough to sneak by without too much discredit. They really don't care. But people doing the same kind of work have achieved greatness—because they cared and took their job seriously, as an important part of their life. This principle applies as much to a stay-at-home mom as to a senator, the mail carrier as to the chairman of the board in the high-rise.

I believe more people should remember what Charles Dickens wrote. "It is well for a man to respect his own vocation, whatever it is, and to think himself bound to uphold it and to claim for it the respect it deserves. No, there are no unimportant jobs. There are only people who treat their work in an unimportant fashion and who must then become unimportant people." As they say in show business, there are no small parts, only small actors.

Every job contains somewhere within it the key to greatness, the road to great achievement, but we've come to think that some jobs or professions are greater than others. That's not true. The person who delivers your cleaning, who does their job in an outstanding fashion, who thinks about their work is a better person and a better professional than the physician who does not approach healthcare in the same way.

People who do their jobs in an outstanding way develop the real kind of security that no one can take away from them. The inner security that comes only from doing whatever is given to you to do in an outstanding manner. These are the people who are seldom hurt or even bothered by recessions and depressions. When times are bad, we can do without people who have made themselves unimportant—but we must have, we need the outstanding people. We depend on them and we know they can be given a job and left alone. We know they will do it well and do even more than they have to, more than they're paid to do. In this way, industry makes a profit on their services and they will always profit from their industry.

Competency

To be your best in your job is an act of will. Actions completed every day over a period of time create competence that will take you to the top. Daily actions develop habits. All habits aren't bad. However, breaking a bad habit and replacing it with a productive, good habit is a requirement if you want to earn what you're worth.

The secret of happiness is freedom, but the secret of freedom, courage.

One of the most interesting things about people is that they can and do change for the better. A person who was once a criminal can become a model citizen. Another person kicks a drug habit and begins living a life of responsibility and contribution. And for every one of those there are millions who over a span of years have become substantially better people—who are kinder, more honest, more conscientious about their responsibilities, and so on.

But just how does a person improve and why?

In his column *Strictly Personal*, Sydney J. Harris, well-known Chicago newspaper columnist, wrote:

> It is not an act of intellect that makes people change themselves for the better. Not a matter of insight, but an act of the will. For intelligence without courage is as static as courage without intelligence is rash. It is intelligence with courage that results in the necessary act of the will we need in order to bring about constructive change in ourselves.
>
> The person who breaks a bad and destructive habit does so by an act of the will. His intelligence tells him that he has a bad habit. It may be a work habit. It may be a steady habit or a non-steady habit. It might be a drug habit. It can be any sort of non-productive or destructive habit. Any person with

a bad habit knows about it. His intelligence informs him.

But changing a bad habit into a good one or at least getting rid of the bad one takes an act of the will over a sufficiently long period of time to render it impotent. After a period of time, a surprisingly short time for most habits, it no longer clamors for attention. It fades away and finally disappears. Now the will can be turned off. The habit is gone. But it is turning on the will to undertake such a task that takes courage.Ancient Greek strategist Thucydides said, "The secret of happiness is freedom and the secret of freedom, courage." When we rid ourselves of unproductive and debilitating habits, we literally free ourselves to that degree. The more bad habits we can get rid of, the freer we become, the happier we become, the better our self-image becomes. The secret of happiness is freedom, but the secret of freedom, courage.

Habits that make us happy we should keep. Habits that lead to unhappiness and illness we should try to muster the courage to end. It's surprising how easily a bad habit is defeated when faced with courage. As Emerson said, "What a new face courage puts on everything."

Focus Points for Wealth & Wisdom

1. How courageous are you to make big plans? Have you considered that your current plans are too small—that you need to enlarge your goals to accomplish even more?

_____

_____

_____

_____

_____

_____

_____

_____

_____

_____

_____

_____

_____

_____

_____

_____

Big Plans

2. Of the four main ways mentioned in the chapter to become wealthy, which one of the four seems doable to you right now? Which one of the four seems out of your reach?

_____

_____

_____

_____

_____

_____

_____

_____

_____

_____

_____

_____

_____

_____

_____

_____

_____

_____

3. In every job there is a key to greatness and great achievement. In your current position, can you identify that key? Will you work toward using that key to improve your lot in life?

_____

_____

_____

_____

_____

_____

_____

_____

_____

_____

_____

_____

_____

_____

_____

_____

_____

3

YOU TOO?

This mini-book is about *The Secret Advantage* that the most interesting and successful people in the world know and live. These are the people who belong to the "top 5 percent." I believe you, too, would like to belong to such a group.

First, let me explain who belongs to this group, and it's right here that you may as well prepare yourself for a shock. I want you to picture a mental image of 100 young people standing in a line. They are all 25 years of age. The world is ahead of them. Each has as much opportunity as the others. They live in one of the richest countries on earth, truly a land of abundance.

Now, enter this question. What will happen to these 100 young people by the time they are 65 years of age? In other words, let's turn the clock ahead 40 years. What do you think will have happened to these 100 people by the time they turn 65? It's an interesting question, isn't it?

Well, the following are the statistics:

- 1 will be rich
- 4 will be independent for life
- 5 will be working
- 36 will be dead
- 54 will be dependent on an agency or other people

So, *only 5 percent of those 100 were financially independent at age 65*. To ask yourself if you want to belong to the top 5 percent is really unnecessary. *Of course* you want to belong, and perhaps you already belong.

When you discovered that only 5 percent of people made the grade financially, were you shocked? You should have been, because this is really a serious indictment.

Look at it this way. If you practice playing the piano 8 hours a day, 40 hours a week, 50 weeks a year for 40 years, I know you'll agree that you would be an accomplished pianist. Or what if you practiced anything 8 hours a day, 5 days a week, 50 weeks a year for 40 years? Medicine, law, selling agriculture, teaching, carpentry, writing, anything at all—in 40 years you can become an expert at anything, right? Of course.

Well, the 54 out of 100 who arrived at age 65 without having become financially independent in a land bursting with abundance had worked in our economy 8 hours a day, 5 days a week, 50 weeks a year for 40 years—yet in that length of time they didn't figure out how to be financially independent for the remaining and certainly the best years of their lives.

Why? How is this possible?

Financial independence is certainly not a matter of luck. It's a simple matter of planning. How much money do you suppose the average person earns in 40 years? Well, going by present statistics, a man of even very average income should earn in excess of $200,000.[1] That's one-fifth of a million dollars. That's a fortune. Where did it all go?

Conformity

While you're pondering this question, let me tell you what the experts say. They say that only 5 percent make the grade because that's the group that does not conform. That's the group that does not follow the crowd. Let's take a quick look at conformity and see what it can mean if we conform—that is, if we act like everybody else, the odds are about 95 to 5 that we'll miss the boat too.

Why do people conform? Well, the late Nobel Prize winning Dr. Albert Schweitzer was asked in London one time, "Doctor, what's wrong with people today?" And

---

1. In 2024, the average American worker made $59,000 per year. Times 40 years would be $2,360,000.

the great doctor replied, "People simply don't think," and that's the answer. People conform because it seems like the easy thing to do and because they've been taught to conform.

From the time they were born and all through school, they were told what to do. They wanted to be liked, to belong to the group. They dressed, played, and acted like the other children. They didn't want to be different because children are sometimes cruel to those who are different. They spent let's say 18 years learning to conform to their group. If they went into military service, they were told what to do again. They must conform.

When those conformists are out of school and on their own for the first time, what's the most natural thing in the world for them to do? Right. They look around to see what others are doing.

Because we've always been told what to do, why should we start thinking for ourselves at age 25? So, most get a job and again, look around to see how the others are doing their jobs. And since it seems to be part of human nature to do no more than a person has to in order to get the weekly paycheck, again, they conform.

Now we know they have 40 years to become great at what they do. Plenty of time, but do they? Not if they follow the crowd, not unless they decide to join the top 5 percent who think and make decisions for themselves.

If we follow the crowd, we haven't got a chance.

46   The Secret Advantage

On the other hand, if we think independently and follow our good ideas with action and stay with it, nothing in the world can keep us from succeeding. You can become financially independent and can see to it that you'll never have to worry about income again as long as you live.

Successful Living

After a number of years since my first record, *The Strangest Secret*, Field Enterprises Educational Corporation asked me to produce a special record for those involved with the *World Book Encyclopedia*[2] and *Childcraft*.

You might like to know that I had been selling *World Book* for years. I got my first set of *World Book Encyclopedia* in 1950 when I began writing and producing my own radio series. I recommended *World Book* enthusiastically not because I was paid to, but because I believed then, as I do now, that it's the most comprehensive, easy-to-use, modern reference material on the market. I have a well-worn set in my library at home and my son received a set of his own for his own room since that's where I had to look whenever I wanted one of mine.

The record turned into this book is a distillation of more than 20 years of research on why some people seem to do so well in life, while others do not. This information has

---

2. The *World Book Encyclopedia* was first published in 1917 and revised annually from 1925. By 1995 World Book was available on CD-ROM and by 1999 available online. World Book has released numerous digital products while continuing to publish its print edition, as of 2024.

Successful living is nothing more than successfully solving problems.

changed my life and the lives of thousands of others who have made the same discovery, and I sincerely hope it will have a happy and profitable effect upon yours. I hope that what you read will make a lasting impression and this information will become a permanent part of your way of life.

To begin, I would like you to remember that *successful people are not without problems.* They have, as a rule, just as many problems and largely the same kind as everyone else. The difference is that *they learn to solve their problems.* Successful living is nothing more than the ability to solve successfully the problems that are as much a part of living as breathing. A vital rule to remember is that *the degree of your success is determined by the extent to which you can solve your problems.*

Now, let me make this statement: If you can tell me what you want, I can tell you how to get it. The problem with the great majority of individuals is not with their ability to achieve their goals in life, but rather their failure to understand two factors vital to successful living:

- The first is to decide and clearly define what we want enough to give it most of our attention until it's been achieved.

- The second is to fully understand that we have the ability to achieve this goal or we wouldn't want it in the first place.

The next vital rule to successful living is to understand that *our success is won or lost by our ability to serve others.* Humans are interdependent, and it's impossible to succeed without serving others—just as it would be impossible to live in our modern world without others serving us. Our rewards in life will and must always be in exact proportion to our service.

Misunderstanding this single law is, in my mind, responsible for fully 90 percent of the frustration and discontent we see around us. In your mind's eye, picture a giant apothecary scale, the kind with the cross arm from which hang two large bowls on chains. One of the bowls is marked *rewards,* the other *service.* These bowls must always be in perfect balance.

Many people don't like this law, if they're even aware of it; but not liking a law does nothing to change it. The basic laws of nature and economics are unchanging. If we're out of step with those basic laws, we are doomed to failure.

Exact Proportion

There are two kinds of rewards or income. One is mental and the other is physical, such as money or property. If a person doesn't like his or her income, all the person has to do is take a good long look at the service he or she is providing. The fact that many individuals in the fields of science, religion, teaching, and so on must measure most of their rewards in the mental (emotional) realm does nothing to alter the fact that their rewards will be in exact proportion to their service.

Wherever you look, you will find this law in undeviating operation. Our rewards will always be in exact proportion to our service. Good examples of this are *World Book* and *Childcraft*. The fact that this is the world's largest publisher of reference material is based solely on the fact that its products have found the widest acceptance and have been sold to more individuals and institutions. This is the law then that lies as the supporting structure of economics and personal well-being for the company. All attempts by employees and staff to sidestep or in any way avoid this law will result in frustration and failure.

This brings up the question, "If what I want is more than I now have, how can I increase my service in order to earn it?"

Answer: Whom do we serve? We serve people, so let's take a moment to try to understand people. The more we understand them, the better we can serve them. I think of an adult human being as a grown child doing his or her best to play for the first and last time on earth this game called life. The extent to which a person learns the rules of this mighty game determines success—but right here we run into an historic and exasperating fact.

You Too? **51**

Our rewards in life will and must always be in exact proportion to our service.

Focus Points for Wealth & Wisdom

1. On a scale from 1 to 10, how would you rate your conformity leanings? If 1 is, "I'm a lone wolf," and 10 is, "I go along to get along," where do you fall within those two extremes? Where will that rating land you 5, 10, 25 years from now according to what you read in the chapter?

_____

_____

_____

_____

_____

_____

_____

_____

_____

_____

_____

_____

2. Do you agree that learning to solve problems means living successfully? How do you most often approach a problem? Ignore it. Ask someone to solve it for you. Set out to solve it yourself.

3. Because every person is dependent on other people, in one way or another, in what ways can you serve those who serve you so that you become more successful as you do the same for them? Write that answer using personal experiences and examples. Are you then willing to follow through with action to improve your financial status, health, family life?

_____

_____

_____

_____

_____

_____

_____

_____

_____

_____

_____

_____

_____

_____

_____

4

95 TO 5 ODDS

People down through the centuries have, with the most amazing consistency, divided themselves into two groups. One group contains about 5 percent of any given population. The other group contains the remaining 95 percent. Neither of these two groups is any better than the other, but one thing separates them. The big group, the one containing about 95 percent of the people, never seems to get the word while the smaller group, the 5 percent, does.

Now, what do I mean by getting "the word"? I mean about 95 percent of people never quite understand emotionally or intellectually that we as individuals control to an altogether unsuspected extent our lives here on earth—that *each one of us is the architect of the structure fashioned by our years.*

You see, all of us want the same things, but only about 5 percent figures out how to get them. I think this fact is perfectly stated in the *World Book* booklet titled *Opportunity Unlimited,* which says, "Within each of us burn two

Within each of us burn two unquenchable ambitions—to serve importantly and to gain financial independence.

unquenchable ambitions—to serve importantly and to gain financial independence." Both of these worthwhile goals are within the reach of all of us, man or woman, but according to statistics only about 5 percent achieve both.

Why? Let's look at it logically. Every human being has a tendency to think, act, and talk like those who surround us. This is our environment, and it exercises an enormous influence on our lives. We've already pointed out that 95 percent don't seem to get, or understand, the word— that they are the architects of their lives.

So it follows that in the case of any given individual, the odds are 95 to 5 that the person is surrounded by the larger group. And since a body in motion tends to remain in motion until acted upon by an outside force, the person will continue to conform to the group unless we can do a better job of serving that individual through knowledge. So, here is our largest opportunity for service, and the rewards will take care of themselves.

Now right here let me restate what we've covered so far. Our rewards—emotional and tangible—will be in proportion to our service. The failure of most people to live successfully is not caused by their lack of abilities, far from it, but rather in their failure to decide what they want and understanding that their wants are governed by their talents and abilities, and that we are divided into two groups of roughly 5 percent and 95 percent. And the 5 percent group is successful.

A Worthy Ideal

Let me give you a definition of success, which to my mind covers the subject completely. *Success is the progressive realization of a worthy ideal; everyone who knows where they are going in life is a success.* The moment you decide what you intend to accomplish, what you consider is a worthy ideal—you are successful. Once the goal has been accomplished, you are again, by our definition, a failure until you establish a new goal toward which to work.

To my mind, this is what we as human beings were intended to do, to go through life from one achievement to another and to finally come to the end of our road here on earth still reaching, still working toward a new and better plateau on which to stand. This is to live and live completely, to know as much as we can know, to serve as much as we can serve, to accomplish as much as we can accomplish.

Since success is the progressive realization of a worthy ideal, why are we faced with only 5 percent who can be called really successful? Because the best estimates available tell us that only about 5 percent will ever decide upon and define the one thing they want—one thing because we can only do one thing at a time. To my mind, the story of a person's life is the story of a quest, a search to which they devote their lives.

We know that the happiest people on earth are those who know exactly what they seek and set boldly out to find it. While we're all dreamers, the fortunate ones have found a dream so exciting and worthwhile that they devote part or all of their lives to making that dream come true.

But while all dream, by far the great majority, that 95 percent, never realizes that a persistent daydream is often the point where we should set our compass, the place toward which we are to journey. The tragedy is that the great majority shrugs off this built-in direction finder and returns to the wide, visible, well-marked road in life they feel must be the best road because it carries the heaviest traffic.

Well, let's make this point clear. The road in life with the heaviest traffic is not the best road to follow, for it is the road of the 95 percent. It is the road with no more opportunity and with 19 times as much competition.

Achievement Secrets

Let me very briefly tell you how I got started on this business of making a study of people and why they wind up the way they do. I spent nearly 20 years looking for the secret to achievement. I didn't know at the time that this topic was older than the pyramids and had appeared in more than 50 million books.

It started in 1933 during the "Great Depression" for me. I was bothered by the difference that existed

95 to 5 Odds   **61**

Success is the progressive realization of a worthy ideal.

between what I had been told and what I could see around me.

For example, I had been told that humans were God's noblest creatures and had dominion over all the earth and all its other creatures. I knew this was true, but in my neighborhood the creatures were eating better than we were, and I wanted to know why so many were poor when there was such abundance on earth. They had no money, but there was still as much as there had been a few years before. Where had it gone? They had little education, yet education was on every side of them. They had very little food, yet it was raised in abundance. They lived in inadequate and ugly dwellings, yet there were good homes for sale.

It was apparent to me that these people didn't have the answer to the problem. They were good people, but they didn't have the answers. They were discouraged and confused in a world that should have been filled with challenge and excitement. It's true that we were in a period of general economic depression; but to the thinking individual, this represents another problem to be solved, another challenge to overcome—and to many it sparked their greatest accomplishments.

I remember reading something once about discouragement. It was a fable about a devil sale and he had his many wares on display. There was the rapier of jealousy, the dagger of fear, the strangling noose of hatred, each with its high price. But on a purple pedestal gleaming dully in the light was a worn and battered wedge. This was the devil's most prized possession and it was not for sale, for with it alone he could stay in business. It was the wedge of discouragement.

As I remember, the people in my neighborhood were incredibly discouraged. Discouragement can only come from one of two things: 1) lack of information, or 2) a situation over which we have no control. It is very seldom that we're faced with number 2. Almost all discouragement can be traced to a lack of information. For example, if you fell from the top of a high building, you could justify discouragement because at that moment you have no control, and it can be traced to you having made the fatal step, which is a lack of information about the law of gravity.

The Answers

When I asked these people why we were in the fix we were in, they answered with a very human response. They blamed other people. They looked everywhere for the answer except where it really was—within themselves. These were the 95 percent.

I decided to find out just what it was that separated the haves from the have-nots—not just in a financial sense, but in every sense. I found the answers in books written by great men—I found the answers in the Bible.

Why didn't the people around me know the answers? They didn't read good books. They didn't read the Bible. Everyone owned one because it was fashionable like a set of Shakespeare, but they didn't read that either. They were discouraged because they lacked information. They didn't know the rules of this game called life. They didn't realize that without a goal, an aiming point, we're without purpose or direction. They clung together, feeling somehow that there was safety in numbers, without realizing that in this case, just the opposite is true. They didn't know that if we conform to the big group, the odds are 95 to 5 that we'll miss the boat that takes us into almost every vital and important aspect of living.

To prove this, you need only take a look at human history. Of all the billions of human beings who've lived on earth, all great advances and all great ideas have come from just a handful, a few thousand out of billions. How have the people as a group reacted to the great ideas? Every great leader and thinker from Socrates to the Wright brothers has been scorned, ridiculed, poisoned, imprisoned, stoned, pilloried, burned at the stake, or crucified.

Humankind as a group has made a consistently grizzly game of tormenting our saviors. Why? Lack of information. Lack of knowledge. It comes from following the wrong crowd. What can we learn from all this as individuals? Two things: 1) to amount to anything as an individual,

*We are what
we think about.*

we have to have individual goals, individual thinking, and take individual action, and 2) we must never conform to the great mass of people.

We must love them and help them—our joy and success is determined by the extent to which we serve them—but we must never lose our individuality and identity by permitting ourselves to be submerged in this suffocating sea of indirection and purposelessness. There's nothing wrong with emulation. In fact, it's a good idea so long as we emulate a person who represents someone we wish to become—but never the crowd, never the 95 percent.

The Secret to Achievement

The secret to achievement that I devoted nearly 20 years to finding was pure simplicity, which caused it to elude me, just as it manages to elude the majority of people in any given age. I had been looking for something complicated, something only a mind prepared by years of study could grasp—and yet I found the answer so simple a child can understand it.

In six words the secret is: *We are what we think about.* Our minds, our thinking controls our destinies here on earth to a degree totally unsuspected by the great majority of people. When you think about it a moment, it becomes so obvious, so clear and simple.

Well then, if we become what we think about and if we can control our minds, we can pretty well tell our own future. That's the point I want to make. That's what I meant when you read earlier that each of us is the architect of the structure fashioned by our years.

This means that if we're confused about what we want to become or accomplish, our lives, our environment will mirror that confusion. It also means that if we know what we seek, it will and must be accomplished. Barring an act of God or catastrophe over which we have no control, we as individuals can call our own shots for the rest of our lives. We can know what it means to go through life from one success to another, to play life according to the rules and reap the rewards. We can know what it means to have peace of mind and live calm, cheerful, successful lives.

You are at this moment the sum total of your thoughts to this point, for there is nothing else you can be—and five years from now you can be and have anything you set your entire mind and heart upon. Now let me tell you of a way you can use this law to accomplish more in five years than the average person does in 40.

Focus Points for Wealth & Wisdom

1. What does being the "architect of your life" mean to you? What are you currently building in your life to make it better. Is there anything you need to tear down to make room for improvements? Any restoration work you need to do?

_____

_____

_____

_____

_____

_____

_____

_____

_____

_____

_____

_____

_____

_____

95 to 5 Odds

2. Do you believe wholeheartedly with the author's definition of success: "Success is the progressive realization of a worthy ideal; everyone who knows where they are going in life is a success"? What is your personal definition of success? Are you working toward becoming and living that definition?

_____

_____

_____

_____

_____

_____

_____

_____

_____

_____

_____

_____

_____

_____

_____

_____

3. "You are at this moment the sum total of your thoughts to this point, for there is nothing else you can be…." How committed are you to calling your own shots for the rest of your life—to setting your thoughts and actions on being the successful, happy person God created you to be?

_____

_____

_____

_____

_____

_____

_____

_____

_____

_____

_____

_____

_____

_____

_____

_____

5

THE FORMULA

From the earliest writings, we know that the human race has been comprised of the haves and the have-nots. As mentioned previously, when I was a kid back during the Great Depression, I was obsessed with the desire to know what invisible something separated the haves from the have-nots. I wanted to know why so few managed to be well-off financially in a country where success is available to everyone.

Even today, for example, in checking the statistical abstract of the United States, published by the Bureau of the Census, I discovered that only 10 percent of men in this country, 65 years of age and older, have incomes of $6,000 or more a year. More than 80 percent of all men, 65 or older, have incomes less than $4,000 a year. Only 7.6 percent have incomes between $7,000 and $10,000 a year, and only 3.7 percent have incomes of $10,000 a year or more.[3]

---

3. According to the US Census Bureau, the median household income for Americans aged 65 and over was $50,290 in 2022 with Social Security income accounting for over half of total income followed by earnings income and pension and retirement account income.

For example, a man starts his working career in his 20s, often earlier. He's fortunate in that he lives in the free world. He has the same opportunities that everyone else has. He has better than 40 years to be financially successful in the richest country on earth. Yet according to the latest statistics, only about 10 out of 100 will be financially secure by the time age 65 rolls around. And only about 4 men out of 100 will be financially comfortable. Why? Well, let me tell you how to find out for yourself.

Conduct your own survey. Start down the street in your neighborhood on any Saturday or Sunday, and ask the man of every house two questions: The first question: *"What are you doing at the present time to increase your income?"* When you've evaluated the blank stare you get in response to that question, ask question number two: *"How much money are you planning to be worth at age 65?"*

When the silence becomes too unnerving, thank him and move on to the next house. Ask 50 men, 100, and 1,000 until you are completely convinced that the reason men don't make any more money during their working lives and the reason men aren't financially independent at age 65 is simply that they seldom, if ever, do any constructive thinking on either subject. It's that simple, unfortunately.

74   The Secret Advantage

Winners All

The reason it's so easy to earn far more money than the average person earns in this country is that so few, so very few, are going about it the right way. This is a race without enough contestants to bother about. The few who are really in the race can all be winners. Some will finish ahead of the others, but even the one who finishes last in this race will be financially secure. Most people, more than 90 percent, aren't even in the race.

To prove it, ask yourself the two survey questions: Up until the time you started reading this book, what were your plans for increasing your income? How much money had you decided to be worth by the time you were age 65?

People who make large incomes aren't lucky and they're not crooks—as those without money are so fond of pretending—nor are they endowed with more brains and talent than their friends and neighbors, nor are they privy to occult secrets, and only a very few were lucky enough to have had rich fathers or grandfathers. No.

Most people earning the big incomes today started the same way you and I did, and most other people. The only difference between those who earn big incomes and those who earn small incomes is that those earning big incomes *decided* to earn more. They made it their business to earn more.

For instance, a woman who doesn't think about baking an apple pie for dinner tonight will never think of looking up the recipe for apple pie. Without the real desire for pie, there's no motivation to get the recipe. A man who doesn't think about driving to Saint Louis, Missouri or Nacogdoches, Texas will never get roadmaps showing what roads to take to get to Saint Louis or Nacogdoches. And anyone who never decides to earn more money will never think of learning how or looking up the process for earning more money.

Excuses and Alibis

People do what they make up their minds to do. So get rid of superstitions and excuses once and for all that people who earn big money are special or lucky or get the breaks or had money to begin with or knew someone or are smarter or anything else. These are alibis and can all be disproved a thousand times.

The reason there are so many alibis around is that people who fail to make the grade financially are seldom honest enough to admit they really didn't try and keep trying. So in order to justify their failure, in order to remain seated, they dream up or pass along these old alibis. We all are self-made, but only the successful will admit it.

I was recently in Charleston, South Carolina. I'd never been there before, so I hired a taxi to drive me around the historic old town. I particularly wanted to see the Battery where that famous shot was fired on Fort Sumter. Along this beautiful drive, some of Charleston's oldest and finest homes look out over the bay. I commented to my aging driver on what lovely homes they were.

He said, "Yeah, some of those homes have 40 rooms." And then he thought a moment and said, "And every one of them is owned by a crook." This is how the have-nots justify themselves and their lot in life. I didn't say anything because I didn't feel I was entitled to advise him or try to straighten out his thinking. This is a free country where, as long as he doesn't hurt others, everyone has the unalienable right to be just as wrong as he wants to be.

My taxi driver and men and women like him all around the world have been kidding themselves and holding themselves down and refusing the bounty and abundance of the world for centuries. Knowledge is available to everyone. We can either listen to those qualified to teach us, or we can go along with those ancient stumbling blocks we get from people who don't know any more than we do. The truth, incidentally, about those homes along that beautiful drive is that they were built by the men and women who made the largest contribution to the city of Charleston and to the country and to the world.

The Formula **77**

Your rewards in life will always be in exact proportion to your contribution, your service.

The Formula

Next, I'm going to give you the formula for getting rich or average or poor. The formula for getting rich also explains why you're in your present position, whether you're earning $6,000 a year, $16,000, or $60,000. It applies to every adult, whether employed or unemployed. It applies to the richest and to the poorest and every person in between. And here it is, again:

That formula is the key. Memorize it. Think about it until you know it emotionally as well as intellectually. It might give you some slight feeling of superiority to realize that there's probably not another person within a mile of where you live who knows it. You can add it as a question on your survey if you want proof of that.

If you want it in another form, here it is as it applies to a person's job—it's the same thing really, but expressed differently: *The money you are paid by the company you work for will always be in direct ratio to the need for what you do, your ability to do it, and the degree of difficulty involved in replacing you.*

Maybe you will want to write down the formula in both of its forms and think about it until it's as much a part of you as your name.

All right, now you have the formula! As you think about it, its meaning will become clearer to you.

With the formula, there are rules that must be applied to properly use it. This formula, together with a set of rules, is your recipe and your roadmap to earning all the money you really want. Now for the important rules, please read the next chapter.

Focus Points for Wealth & Wisdom

1. Have you decided to make it your business to earn more? If not, what are some of your excuses? Alibis?

_____

_____

_____

_____

_____

_____

_____

_____

_____

_____

_____

_____

_____

_____

_____

_____

_____

2. Are you a self-made success? What steps are you willing to take to make it so?

3. "The money you are paid by the company you work for will always be in direct ratio to the need for what you do, your ability to do it, and the degree of difficulty involved in replacing you." True?

6

WORKABLE FORMULA RULES

So now let's look at a set of rules that are part of workable formula—rules for this game of life that cannot fail to take us to where we wish to go.

The first and most important thing to remember is the rule that controls our life, which is: *we become what we think about.* This means *we must establish a worthwhile goal to work toward,* a goal that will occupy our minds most of the time. This goal should be written out or illustrated. We should look at it and *restate our purpose* every morning, every night, and as many times during the day as we can.

We must fully understand emotionally as well as intellectually that whatever it is we set our heart upon will become real in our lives. We must also remember the law that lies as the basic foundation for all economics and personal well-being as well: our *rewards will be in exact proportion to our service.* And if we want to get into the top 5 percent of the people who are successful, we must often cut ourselves away from the effects of our environment and become individuals with individual goals, individual thinking, individual actions.

We must realize that *our daily work contains opportunities*—more opportunities than we could develop in a lifetime. And that our job contains within itself the key to greatness, the road to everything we could possibly want in life for ourselves and our families. We must realize too that *security can be found inside.* Security is found in one place only—inside of us. If it isn't there, it isn't anywhere. And the only road to security lies in doing what we do for a living surpassingly well.

Also, we must *become professionals* at what we do and that becoming a pro involves knowledge, planning, and working. Knowledge of what we sell, who we sell, and selling. Planning by establishing the goal, which automatically establishes our work pattern. The great salesman is like the great golfer. It looks easy the way he does it because it is easy the way he does it. But it took time, dedication, and work in its accomplishment. Is it worth it? You bet it is.

Two Ambitions

Remembering that the definition of success is the progressive realization of a worthy ideal, what's the ideal toward which you are working now, today, yesterday, and tomorrow? Can you write it in one sentence?

Is your goal sharply and clearly defined? Now for a moment, let's return to the quote, "Within each of us burn two unquenchable ambitions: 1) to serve importantly and 2) to gain financial independence." The first of these two desirable ambitions you've already achieved by now realizing that all jobs are important and serving to the best of your ability is vital in reaching and accomplishing your goals.

Now let's take a look at the second ambition, *financial independence*. I mentioned previously that I could tell you how in five years you can be and have anything you set your mind on—and that every job holds the key to everything you want in life, but you must look for it and think on it.

Since only about 5 percent make it to financial independence, we must take serious steps to place ourselves in this percentage group. We can do this by making two decisions. The first is to decide once what you're going to do for a living—that will be your career. Since your opportunities are unlimited and your options are constantly growing with our dynamic economy and our exploding population,[4] this is an important decision.

Being undecided and uncommitted about what you are going to do prevents you from doing your best. You're working with one hand and looking around with

---

4. The US population in 1945 was 140 million. During the "baby boom" years—1946-1964—more than 76 million babies were born, an increase of more than 50 percent (www.britannica.com/topic/baby-boomers; accessed August 13, 2024).

Workable Formula Rules **87**

the other. As a result, neither is done satisfactorily. And remember, your work contains within it the road to greatness, the key to anything you want for yourself and your family.

Hundreds of people have already proved this fact, so choose your career path. Once this decision has been made, you will feel as though a weight has been lifted from your mind. Perhaps for the first time in your life, you will know where you are in the world. You now have a place where you can serve, where you're needed and respected, where what you're doing is important.

After this decision has been made, we come to the second decision to make. Devote yourself to become a professional at whatever job you chose. You can either compete or create. If you compete with all the other people in your line of work, you must be willing to accept the same rewards. If that's what you want, fine. But if you want to become a professional at what you do, then you must create. And when you do this, there's no limit to what you can achieve.

Job Security

Everyone wants job security, but this concept is impossible. There is no such thing as a job that represents security. Anyone with a job can lose it for any one of a thousand reasons at any time.

Those people I saw back in 1933 demoralized and afraid thought that a job represented security. And when it was taken from them, they lost everything. They found themselves lost in a world they didn't understand. A job cannot represent security, financial or otherwise. There is only one place on earth you can find security—inside yourself. If you have security inside where it belongs, your spouse and children can feel it when you sit down to eat with them and they're warmed by it.

When you have security inside where it belongs, others can see it when you're walking down the street and feel it when you enter a room—that security and confidence can't be taken away from you. Even if you lose your money, home, and cars, if you have a family willing to start over, and most of them are, within a year you can be doing just as well as before the losses.

You can't keep a good, hard-working person down no matter what happens. Like cream on milk, you can shake it all day, but just set it down for a while and it will bounce right to the top again. Confidence and security come from doing what you do for a living surpassingly well. It comes from being a professional in a world of amateurs. Becoming a pro isn't difficult. It comes from knowing what to do with time. It comes from knowledge, planning, and working.

Whatever your goal may be, write it down in detail....And you will reach more successful ports in a few years than most people do in a lifetime.

Knowledge, Planning, Working

First, *knowledge*. Knowledge means learning everything we can about your product or service—what you make, sell, offer, whatever your chosen profession is. Knowledge is also learning everything possible about who buys your product or service. Also, learning everything you can about selling and marketing.

Knowledge and learning just those three subjects would fill a large library, but we can take our lessons one at a time; by devoting an hour a day to study, we can become outstanding professionals in five years or less. And professionals can write their own paychecks. Good times or bad. And professionals can live where and work when they choose.

Second, *planning*. Planning means writing down the specific goal you're working toward. It means writing in detail about the first port of call you want to reach, realizing that you can only reach one at a time. Planning means selecting the income that represents financial independence to you. Once this amount has been selected, you know exactly what you must do to reach it. As soon as our first goal has been reached, we can set a new one. Good things will happen to you. The so-called breaks start coming your way—but they are actually a result of planning and working positively that attracts good things to you.

I can't emphasize too much the importance of describing your goal in detail. If your goal is to live in a beautiful new home, get the actual plans or at least an elevation drawing of the home and carry it with you so that you can look at it regularly. If your goal is to bring home a certain amount of money a month, write down the specific amount for the coming year to the penny—and then work your plan. Whatever your goal may be, write it down in detail. Then you, like the ship, are on course! And you will reach more successful ports in a few years than most people do in a lifetime.

And third, *working*. To achieve more than average results means working more than the average, of course. But with knowledge and proper planning, it will seem easy. Moreover, to work you need energy. And energy is inextricably linked to desire. Unless you have a strong desire, you won't have the energy. Once your goal has been crystallized in your mind and you realize that you become what you think about, your doubts vanish as to whether or not you can achieve your desired ends. And with the picture of your dream in your mind, you have abundant energy to keep moving forward toward your goal!

Focus Points for Wealth & Wisdom

1. Have you established a worthwhile goal to work toward—one that will occupy your mind most of the time? Have you concluded that whatever you set you heart on will become real in your life?

_____

_____

_____

_____

_____

_____

_____

_____

_____

_____

_____

_____

_____

_____

_____

_____

2. Have you realized that confidence and security is found in within you, that doing every job and serving to the best of your ability will give you everything you want in life?

3. How important are *knowledge, planning, and working* to you regarding your career, your business, your life?

_____

_____

_____

_____

_____

_____

_____

_____

_____

_____

_____

_____

_____

_____

_____

_____

_____

_____

_____

_____

7

FROM BEGINNING-TO-END PERSPECTIVE

Now let's look at the big picture calmly and analytically. Since statistics prove that only 5 percent become financially independent in a country where there's more than enough to go around, the 95 percent must be doing something wrong. And what do leading experts and educators say is wrong with most people today? They just don't think for themselves. They simply do not look at life from a beginning-to-end perspective. They don't see their lives as having a beginning, a middle, and an end.

As someone who wants to be in the top 5 percent group, you will take thinking seriously. You won't conform to the 95 percent way of thinking because that means you will miss the financial boat. You must think now before it's too late. I encourage you to think about the following principles.

Work and Money

There are only two methods that can contribute to financial success: 1) *the work you do for a living;* and 2) *the money you save.* Only by saving money can it be accumulated and put to work for you. By logically following through the whole of life step by step, we get rid of all confusion, doubt, and guesswork, and we're left with just two jobs that anyone can handle. One, the work we do for a living, and two, the money we can save.

Now let's take them in order. First, the job. Naturally, I have no way of knowing what it is you do for a living or what your circumstances happen to be, but more than twenty years of research have proved one thing. No matter what your job may be at this moment, it contains the road to greatness if handled correctly. As mentioned previously and worth saying again, *every job is loaded with hidden opportunities.* From checking hats to laying bricks, from working in a factory to selling shoes, whether you work for someone else or for yourself, there is hidden in your daily work more opportunity than you can develop in a lifetime—if you look for it.

How many ideas do you think would come to mind in a single day if you really started to think? Five, twenty, a hundred? Have you ever stopped to think that one idea can make you rich? How do you think your job will be handled ten years from now? Can you do it that way now? What improvements will be made in your industry during the next fifty years? You know that improvements are inevitable. Someone comes up with them. Why not you? Do you know as much about your job or business as the CEO of a major corporation or an award-winning athlete knows about their field of endeavor? You really should, you know.

Have you given the same work and dedication to your job that an attorney has given to the study of law? Whatever you have chosen to do for a living is your profession. There's no such thing as one job or profession being more honorable or better than any other. It's all in the way we look at the overall arch of our lives and our work. Our attitude makes the difference, a huge difference.

How long do you think it would take you to know everything there is to know about your job and its application to your industry and our economy as a whole? Five years? You realize that if you attacked your job for the next five years the same way you would have to if you were working for yourself, that you can be a national expert on your particular job in five years? You can become an expert on any one particular subject in five years—and it's the experts in this country who become wealthy. The experts think the ideas into reality. The experts are constantly in demand regardless of economic cycles.

Your mind is a great and largely unexplored continent. You own it and no one else can trespass upon it. We know it contains unbelievable riches, but they must be found. And there's only one way to explore and prospect

From Beginning-to-End Perspective   **99**

Your mind is a great and largely unexplored continent. You own it and no one else can trespass upon it.

a human mind—you must think. Like any other kind of prospecting, it takes time and dedication, but of this you can be absolutely certain. If you do your job to the very best of your ability and think constantly of ways it can be done better, you will immediately belong to the top 5 percent and your ideas will definitely guarantee you a great future.

Now you might say, "Why should I knock myself out for the company I work for?" This is what the majority of workers say—and remember, it's the majority that always has and unfortunately probably always will miss the boat in life.

You are actually only working for yourself. Each day, you're building the house you and your family must live in, and the materials and construction you put into your house will determine its strength and your degree of greatness. Remember that no matter what you're now doing for a living, it contains the key to greatness if you look for it until you find it. So much for the importance of your job—now on to the other method to becoming financially independent.

Saving Systematically

The second point that guarantees your being in the top 5 percent with those who achieve financial independence concerns the money you save systematically until you are independent. The men and women who find themselves financially independent at 65 didn't suddenly come into an inheritance on their 65th birthday. They planned it that way and then stuck to their plan. Saving money is the only check you can write that doesn't cost you a penny.

You have probably seen a bricklayer starting on a large building. He puts down the first brick and you think, *My gosh, what a huge job.* But one day you drive by and there's the building all finished. The first brick is still there way down at the bottom, and all the other bricks are in their places. If he hadn't put down the first brick, none of the others could have been put in place. Each brick, small though it is, makes a vital contribution to the finished structure—and it's the same with saving money.

Unless you're saving at least 10 percent, preferably more, of what you now earn, you're making an extremely serious mistake. Unless you pay yourself at least 10 cents out of each dollar you earn, you are stealing from yourself what can be the most beautiful years of your life, the later years, when you can do everything you always wanted to do. Financial success has nothing at all to do with the money you earn, but only with the money you save.

Life's Inevitabilities

Thinking about life having a start, middle, and end, let's look at what can happen in the middle—and prepare for it.

Have you ever noticed how well women deal with day-to-day family emergencies? I have. It's because most women seem to have a special talent for defending their families against all kinds of real or imagined emergencies. Everything from bruised knees to injured egos. Yet all too often, women are ill-prepared to deal with financial emergencies, the kind of emergencies that would arise if something happened to her spouse. Let me tell you about one smart man.

This man recognized his wife might someday face a financial emergency, so he took steps to avert it, steps you may want to take too. Let's call him Mr. Wilson. Mr. Wilson had a $200,000 estate. He wanted to be sure that if he were incapacitated or should die, his wife and children would be able to maintain their present standard of living—even more than that, to better themselves if possible.

He knew what would happen if he left all his property outright to his wife. At the time of this writing, federal estate taxes would claim $4,800. "That's not too bad," he figured, "considering the size of my estate." And he was right—in fact, the taxes at his death would be quite reasonable, thanks to a special legal provision

From Beginning-to-End Perspective **103**

dealing with the estates of married persons. Probably you already know about it. It's called the marital deduction. But marital deduction or not, Mr. Wilson knew his wife would inherit more than his money. She'd inherit the problems of managing his estate, problems of taxation, accounting, investment in business, problems for which she had no special training.

Actually, few people have the ability, knowledge, experience, and time to manage property competently. Many widows and minor children are unskilled in this field. What's more, Mr. Wilson knew that when his wife died, an additional federal estate tax of $31,260 would have to be paid on her $195,000 inheritance—a much larger tax this time, because the marital deduction would no longer apply.

So what would this leave for the children? The total estate would be cut by at least $36,060. $36,060 would've gone down the drain, because of federal estate taxes alone. Fortunately for the Wilsons, this will never come to pass, because Mr. Wilson established a *revocable living trust*. Now, the total tax on property left to his children will be only $9,600 instead of $36,060—a savings of $26,460.

Actually, the family's savings will be even greater, because now that the bulk of the Wilson's assets are in living trust, they'll be exempt from probate. And remember how costly probate proceedings can be—anywhere from 5 to 10 percent of the total estate, and possibly one to three years of red tape and delay. Such savings are impressive certainly. But don't forget, Mr. Wilson created a living trust for reasons other than tax savings. He wanted to be sure his wife and family would always have expert financial guidance to minimize losses and assure protection of his lifetime savings.

And by setting up a trust during his lifetime, he has the opportunity to observe the efficiency of his trustee, to see his trust in action, and to alter the trust in any way he chooses to fit his objectives or his family's needs.

As a further benefit, he himself can enjoy the income and rewards of sound investment management for the rest of his life. He can free himself from the burden of bookkeeping and tax accounting problems. He's relieved of the details and concerns that his personal management of the state entailed.

Now, having learned some of the advantages of living trusts, perhaps you're wondering, as I wondered, why more people don't create them. Well, I concluded that it's because most people make two mistakes. See if you agree with me first: most people never sit down and add up all of their assets. Therefore, they never realize how much they're worth, and how much they stand to lose in the way of unnecessary taxes and estate settlement costs. Second, human nature being what it is, people tend to procrastinate. So some people, even if they do realize how much they have to lose, put off estate planning until the tomorrow that never comes.

From Beginning-to-End Perspective **105**

I hope you don't make these mistakes. They can be extremely costly mistakes for you and your family. To take the first step in planning your financial security, inventory your assets. The figures don't have to be exact, it's just an estimate, but add them up and look at the total. You'll probably see you're worth much more than you thought you were. And remember, the larger your estate, the greater your potential savings through a living trust. On the other hand, the smaller your estate, the greater your need to avoid unnecessary loss.

Regardless of the size of your estate, your family's future depends on it. It's up to you to make the most of it. Of course you need expert help, and this is why it's so important to take a second step. Search for a consultant, an expert in estate planning and find a suitable candidate to be your trustee.

But where do you find such a person? Well, you could advertise in the newspaper. Your ad might read this way: "Wanted: Person to assume complete responsibility for planning and managing my estate for me and my family. Must be thoroughly experienced in business management, finance, taxes, accounting, estate laws, and investments. Year-round service required, no vacation, no sick leave, very moderate pay."

Now just how many qualified applicants would answer your ad? Probably not even one, because I think you'll agree that the job demands are too great and the reward's too small to attract the caliber of help you seek.

Yet there is a qualified applicant for this job. It's not only one individual, it's a team. One is your lawyer and the other is the trust department of your bank. Your bank is an institution that makes a business of trusteeship, an institution with a staff of specialists in trustee services, in financial and investment services, in protecting assets, managing money, and minimizing losses. These specialists have had years of experience in highly specialized areas. And they will welcome the opportunity to share their knowledge and experience with you, to explain the ways trust services might very well help meet your particular needs and objectives.

There is one point, however, that I must make quite clear. Trust officers do not advise you what to do in regard to estate planning. That is considered practicing law, which is an attorney's expertise. Your lawyer will give you skilled legal advice and counsel on estate planning, making recommendations specifically tailored for you and your family. Perhaps it'll be a living trust.

Then again, depending on what you tell the attorney, it could be a testamentary trust, or tax saving gifts during your lifetime, or simply changes in your will, or a combination of these alternatives. But whatever the recommendation, you have the assurance of knowing it's the best plan for you and your family in the opinion of an expert regarding the best plan for minimizing taxes, reducing administrative costs and delays, and conserving the estate you've worked so hard to build.

While both your attorney and your trust officer are happy to make their skill and knowledge available to you, you have to suggest the idea to them. Then they make suggestions you can accept or reject as you see fit. Setting up and administering a trust is a team job. You, your attorney, and the trust officer working together. This is a very personal service, and the experience and knowledge these experts have might be just as helpful to you as the advice that helped Mr. Wilson.

It isn't too important which of these experts you talk with first, but you will certainly want to talk with both. What *is* important is that you don't make the mistake so many people do, and do nothing. So I encourage you to think about it and then take these two important steps as soon as possible.

First, complete an inventory of your assets, then call your trust officer or attorney for an appointment, an appointment that could be the wisest investment of time you'll ever make. Just an hour or two might pay off in thousands of dollars in savings. It did for Mr. Wilson. Why not see what it can do for you?

Focus Points for Wealth & Wisdom

1. If you attacked your current job for the next five years the same way you would have to if you were working for yourself, what changes would you have to make? Would it be worth it to improve your status, your financial situation?

2. How savvy are you about saving money? Are you saving at least 10 percent of you earn? "Financial success has nothing at all to do with the money you earn, but only with the money you save." Do you agree?

3. Have you thought about and taken steps to ensure your family's financial security when the inevitable end arrives? There are many issues to consider—and the sooner the better for the sake of your loved ones.

8

ESTABLISHING THE DESTINATION

By now at the end of this book, you realize that succeeding in life has always been a matter of doing what the great majority does not do. Now let's keep this in mind as we get into this business of goals. It isn't that I want to make an odious comparison between the 5 percent and the 95 percent. Not at all. That's just the way it is. And if we don't recognize it, it'll be to our disadvantage. And after all, this book is about *the secret advantage* that will be to your ultimate benefit and gain.

At the beginning of this book, I made the statement, *If you can tell me what you want, I can tell you how to get it.* The trick is not in *achieving* our goals—it is in *establishing* them. A ship would never leave the harbor if it didn't have a destination. An industrial plant would never open its gates if it didn't have a product or a purpose. Football would not be played without goal posts, nor would baseball without a home plate. Every business operates for a purpose. Every game has a reason.

Returning to the analogy of our ship, if you were to climb to the navigation bridge and ask the captain the name and location of his next port of call, he would tell you immediately; there's not the slightest doubt in his mind. Can *you* tell someone your destination just as quickly and in one sentence?

The captain of the ship knows that he can arrive at only one port at a time. He knows that it's impossible to arrive at two. Do *you* know that? He also knows that his destination will be invisible for fully 99 percent of his voyage, but he knows it's there and that he'll reach it, barring an unforeseen catastrophe, if he keeps doing certain things a certain way every day. One fine morning, his destination will appear on the horizon. He'll sail into port as his voyage has been successfully completed.

When the captain's business has been accomplished, he will then sail to another predetermined port of call—and this pattern of progress will take him and his ship from one success to another for the rest of his life.

By understanding that he can reach only one port at a time, the ship's captain can—in the short span of a very few years—reach hundreds of ports successfully. There'll be problems, but each will be solved and the ship and its captain will steam its solitary course over the deep oceans of the world, devoting life to accomplishing the mission and contributing its share to the welfare and economy of the world.

Men and women who follow this sensible, obvious, and meaningful way of life will do the same. But the paradox is that most people are like ships without rudders. They are subject to the whims of wind and tide. And while they hope they will one day arrive in a rich and bustling port, we know that for every narrow harbor entrance, there's a thousand miles of treacherous and rocky coastline.

The chances of a ship just drifting into port are a thousand to one. These are the unfortunate people who, not knowing the rules, believe that circumstance controls their lives. They believe in luck and superstitions, fate, the breaks—they believe that success comes as a result of *who* you know, not *what* you know.

And while they cling to their false alibis, life passes them by, for the rules of life are just and steady, clear, and balanced—and without remorse.

Now what about you?

Let me quote from William James's essay on vital reserves, "Compared with what we ought to be, we are only half awake. Our fires are damped, our drafts are checked. We're making use of only a small part of our possible mental and physical resources. Stating the thing broadly, the human individual thus lives usually far within his limits. He possesses powers of various sorts which he habitually fails to use. He energizes below his maximum and he behaves below his optimum." And then he wrote, "Excitements, ideas, and efforts in a word are what carry us over the dam."

The trick is not in achieving our goals—it is in establishing them.

He goes on in this excellent essay to point out that we have deep reservoirs of abundant energy that we have habitually fail to use. And that by pushing past the first false feeling of fatigue, we will find an exhilarating second wind that will take us to our goals.

This is why in studying the lives of the world's great men and women, I found they seem to be indefatigable. Work meant nothing to them because what they were doing and where they were going filled their entire worlds.

Frequently people find it difficult to establish a goal toward which to work. Realizing that we cannot be successful without a goal, here's a good way to solve the problem. Go off by yourself to somewhere you can think without being disturbed. Then write on a sheet of paper a complete description of the person you would like to become including personality, traits, skills, attitude, style, appearance—everything that comes to mind.

After you write this description, start acting the part of the person you wish to become. Carry, as often as you can, a clear mental image of the person you want to be and begin to be that person. Soon this will become so knit with habit it will lead you without fail to the goal you seek. When you do this, you are using your greatest power—your mind. Remember, *you become what you think about.*

Establishing the Destination **117**

Thinking Your Way Ahead

Sometime ago I was flying west and reading a copy of a television play by the three-time Pulitzer prize-winning playwright, Archibald McLeish. The play was *The Secret of Freedom*. Suddenly I read a line that shook me to the soles of my feet; and for a long time I stared out the window thoroughly digesting the line I had just read. Here is that line: "The only thing about a man that is a man is his mind. Everything else you can find in a pig or a horse." Think about that line until you know what it means.

The only thing that sets us apart as human beings is our divine minds. Everything that has meaning to us—love for our families, our faith, our dreams, our talents and abilities—everything we know is connected to us solely through our minds. Our minds represent our hope and our future.

Yet as a rule, our own mind is the last place the average person turns to for hope and help. Your mind contains riches beyond belief, but you must prospect this rich and largely unexplored continent. And the only way it can be prospected is by systematic study and systematic thinking. Your mind is like a muscle. It will develop only to the extent that you use it—no more.

By devoting an hour a day to study, you are building your mind into a powerful and creative servant. If you devote one hour a day for five days a week, it comes to 260 hours a year. That's 1,300 hours in five years, or the

118   The Secret Advantage

equivalent of 162 eight-hour days devoted to study and research. Believe me, if you do this, in five years you will be one of the most accomplished professionals in your field—and you'll have the world on a string.

You will virtually be able to write your own ticket. The average person works eight hours a day, about 50 weeks a year, for 40 years. That's time enough to become great at anything you want to be. The time will pass anyway. You might as well reap the rewards.

Focus Points for Wealth & Wisdom

1. From all the wisdom gleaned from this book, have you now a clear, one-sentence description of your success destination? Write it and establish it in your mind.

2. Sailing through life comes with solvable problems, settling issues, and standing strong in the winds that may temporarily blow you off course. How committed are you to forging forward to reach your goal?

3. In a few brief paragraphs, can you describe what the *Secret Advantage* means to you as a thinking individual, a devoted spouse/parent, a committed employee, and a contributing citizen of a great nation?

ABOUT EARL NIGHTINGALE

Earl Nightingale (1921–1989) was a man of many talents and interests—nationally syndicated radio personality, entrepreneur, philosopher, US Marine, and more. One thread united all his pursuits—a passion for excellence and living a meaningful existence.

Earl Nightingale's life began simply. He grew up in Long Beach, California. His parents had little money, and his father disappeared when he was 12. But even as a boy, Earl was always asking questions, always reading books in the local public library, wanting to understand the way life works.

Stationed aboard the battleship USS Arizona, Earl Nightingale was one of a handful of survivors when that ship was destroyed and sank at Pearl Harbor. After being separated from the Marine Corps and starting with practically nothing, over the next ten years he founded and headed four corporations. In addition, he wrote, sold, and produced fifteen radio and television programs per week.

Nightingale appeared on all major radio networks. For four years he was the star of the dramatic series *Sky King,* which was carried on more than 500 stations of the Mutual Radio Network. He also began an insurance agency, and in twelve months led it from last to sixth place in the nation with one of the world's largest companies.

The Nation's Press carried the astounding story of the phenomenally successful young man who, at age 35, had become financially independent. He produced his famous recording of *The Strangest Secret,* revealing how anyone can make the most of his or her own capabilities and can attain a rich full measure of success and happiness, right in his or her present job or position. Its theme: "How to achieve greater success and enjoy greater happiness and peace of mind."

At the time, this inspiring recording broke sales records, selling in the multimillions to major industries, retailers and salespeople, clubs and associations, parents, students, and people in virtually all walks of life. His masterful recording has been adapted into books and videos.

OTHER BOOKS IN
THE STRANGEST SECRET
SERIES
by Earl Nightingale

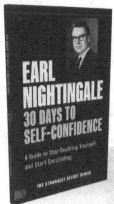 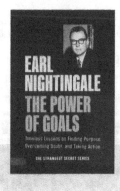 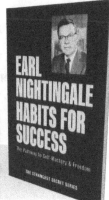

30 Days to Self-confidence:
A Guide to Stop Doubting Yourself and Start Succeeding

The Power of Goals:
*Timeless Lessons on Finding Purpose,
Overcoming Doubt, and Taking Action*

Habits For Success:
The Pathway to Self-Mastery and Freedom

AVAILABLE WHEREVER BOOKS ARE SOLD
WWW.SOUNDWISDOM.COM

THANK YOU FOR READING THIS BOOK!

If you found any of the information helpful, please take a few minutes and leave a review on the bookselling platform of your choice.

BONUS GIFT!

Don't forget to sign up to try our newsletter and grab your free personal development ebook here:

soundwisdom.com/classics